Y0-CUY-096

A MACDONALD BOOK
© Annie West 1987
First published in Great Britain in 1987
by Macdonald & Company (Publishers) Ltd
London & Sydney
A BPCC plc company

All rights reserved

Printed and bound in Great Britain by
Purnell Book Production Limited
Member of the BPCC Group

Macdonald & Company (Publishers) Ltd
Greater London House
Hampstead Road
London NW1 7QX

British Library Cataloguing in Publication Data
West, Annie
  Brinkworth Bear's opposites book.
  1. English language—Synonyms and antonyms—Juvenile literature
  I. Title
  428.1   PE1591

  ISBN 0-356-11805-3

Editor: Valerie Hunt-Taylor
Production: Marguerite Fenn

Brinkworth Bear's Opposites Book

Annie West

Macdonald

long

short

in

out

hot

cold

up

down

big

small

heavy

light

high

low

asleep

awake

hard

soft

full

empty

open

closed

wet

dry

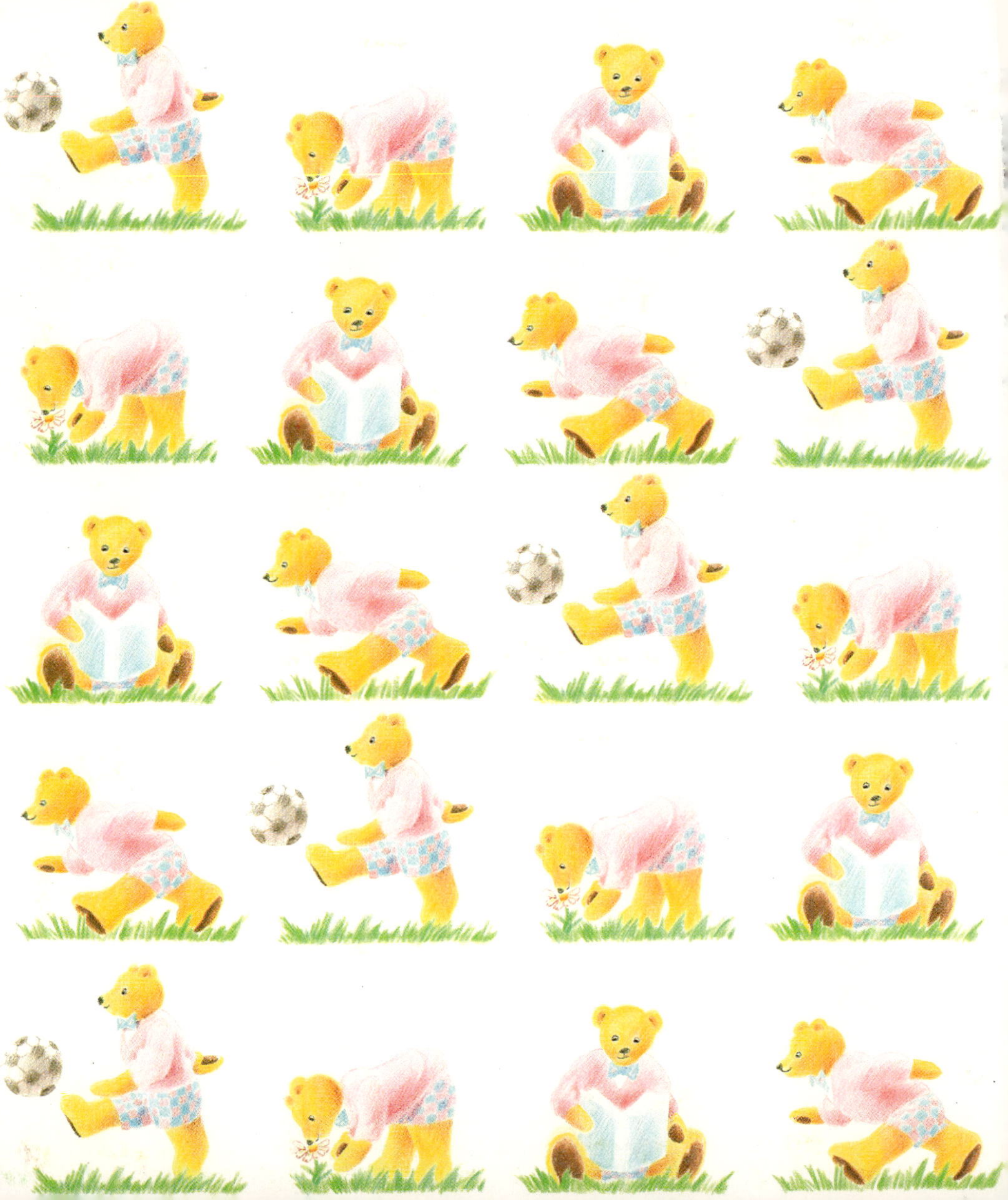